FIRST SPORT

MARTIAL ARTS

James Nixon

Photography by Bobby Humphrey

W

FRANKLIN WATTS
LONDON · SYDNEY

First published in 2014
by Franklin Watts

Franklin Watts
338 Euston Road
London NW1 3BH

Franklin Watts Australia
Level 17/207 Kent Street
Sydney, NSW 2000

Series Editor: Julia Bird
Planning and production by Discovery Books Ltd
Editor: James Nixon
Series designer: Ian Winton
Commissioned photography: Bobby Humphrey
Picture credits: Shutterstock: pp. 2 (Lucian Coman),
3 (Apollofoto), 4 (Pavel L Photo and Video),
6 (PhotoStock10), 7 top (joyfull), 7 bottom (Luis Louro),
13 bottom (Ilya Andriyanov), 15 top (Attl Tibor), 19 (testing).

The author, packager and publisher would like to thank
Bradford Judo Club: www.bradfordjudoclub.co.uk;
Leeds Karate Academy: www.lka.org.uk; and NTX Taekwondo Schools:
www.ntx-schools.net, for their help and participation in this book.

Every attempt has been made to clear copyright.
Should there be any inadvertent omission please apply
to the publisher for rectification.

Dewey number 796.8
ISBN: 978 1445 1 2631 9
Library ebook ISBN: 978 1445 1 2635 7

Printed in China

Franklin Watts is a division of Hachette Children's Books,
an Hachette UK company.
www.hachette.co.uk

Contents

The martial arts

Martial arts are exciting sports where you fight **opponents** one-on-one.

In many martial arts, the aim is to strike your opponent with your hands or feet.

OPPONENT
a person who is on the opposite side in a game

In other martial arts, opponents **grapple** with each other. Lots of people do martial arts to get fit and to learn ways to defend themselves.

GRAPPLE
a fight where opponents grip each other

5

Judo

In judo you have to grapple with your opponent. The aim is to throw them to the floor. The better the throw, the more points you score.

ROU
ESP

RAMIRE

-66 kg 3 13

If your opponent lands on their back, the match ends and you win!

6

Judo matches last up to five minutes and take place on a mat. This stops players hurting themselves when they fall.

JUDOGI the cotton jacket and trousers worn in a judo match

The only kit you need is an outfit called a **judogi**, which is tied at the waist with a belt.

Judo: throws and trips

There are many different judo throws. A player can use their hips (left) or legs (below) to lift their opponent up and throw them onto the mat.

An important skill in judo is to make your moves at the right time. If you wait until your opponent is **off-balance**, you can then trip them to the floor with your leg.

OFF-BALANCE not balanced and at risk of being knocked over

Judo: groundwork

Judo players often end up grappling on the ground. A clever move is to drop down onto your back and throw your opponent over with your legs.

On the ground a player can try
to **pin** their opponent down.

PIN
hold someone
down firmly so they
are unable to move

If you can hold down
your opponent in the same
position for 25 seconds, you win.

Karate: punching and kicking

Punching is the most important skill in karate. Punches should be made with a straight arm and travel from your hip towards the target.

There are many kicks to learn. A front kick is fast and can push an opponent back.

By spinning on one foot, you can kick powerfully with your other foot sideways and backwards.

Taekwondo

The name taekwondo means 'way of the foot and the fist'.

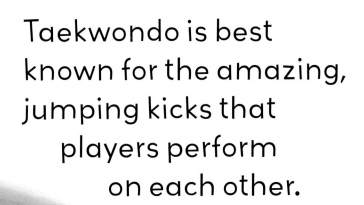

Taekwondo is best known for the amazing, jumping kicks that players perform on each other.

In a taekwondo match, players wear guards on their chest and head. These guards have coloured target areas on them. To score points you must hit the targets on your opponent.

Taekwondo: flying kicks

In taekwondo kicks are more useful than punches. Legs can reach further than arms and are more likely to find the target.

All kicks begin with a bent knee. Then the leg is **thrust** out suddenly with power.

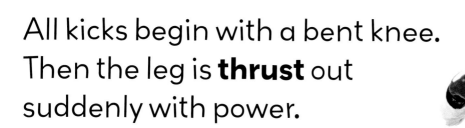

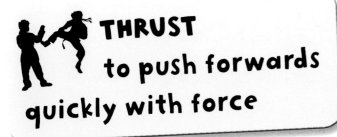

THRUST to push forwards quickly with force

With a short run-up, spectacular flying kicks can be carried out with both feet off the floor.

Index